Catalina Plays The What?

Written By
Antonia Aviles

Illustrated By
Jasmine T. Mills

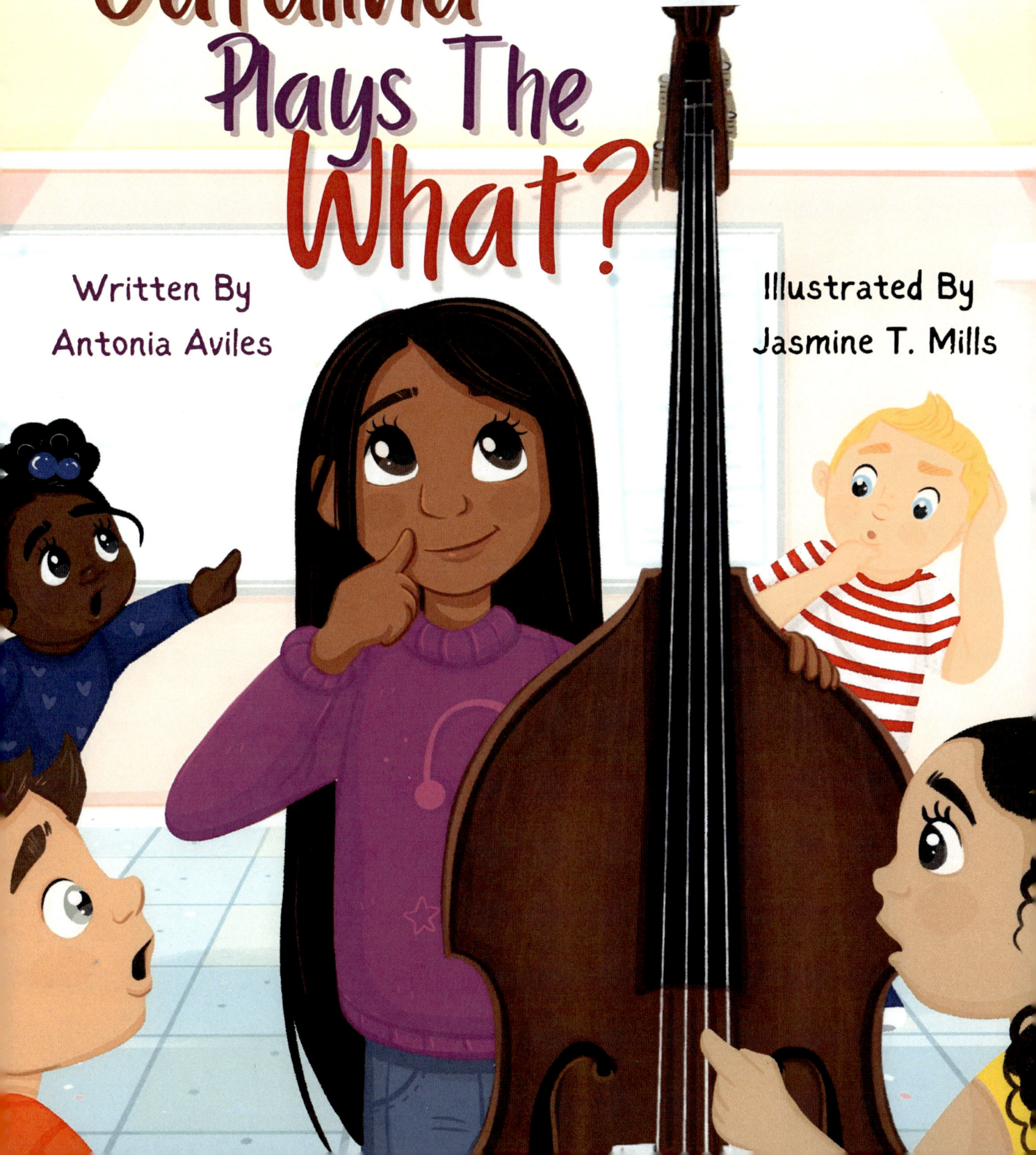

Title: Catalina Plays The What?

Author: Antonia Aviles

Illustrator: Jasmine T. Mills

Dedicated to my husband.

Thank you for sharing your passion and knowledge of double basses for the next generation to enjoy!

Catalina sneaks a peek into her classroom through the window on the door. It is almost time for her big presentation! She rubs her sweaty palms on her sweatshirt and takes a very deep breath. "They are going to love it, right Grandpa?" she asks nervously.

"Yes, honey," he says with a big smile. "Don't worry, you will do great and I'm here for you," he says, winking his right eye at her.

She peeks back inside the classroom just as her teacher waves excitedly for her to come in. Catalina's heart starts pounding. "Ready Grandpa?" she asks.

"WE sure are!" says her grandfather, giving her another wink. Catalina loves his winks. They always make her feel so warm and fuzzy inside.

He opens the door and they enter the classroom.

Last month, the teacher announced that there would be a show-and-tell day in their classroom and Catalina's heart had skipped a beat with excitement. She knew immediately that this would be the perfect chance for her to share her passion for the most incredible instrument in the whole wide world-the double bass!

The day has finally arrived! She has been practicing for this presentation with her grandpa daily. "I can do this," she says to herself quietly as she walks a bit lop-sided from the weight of the double bass she is carrying to the front of the class.

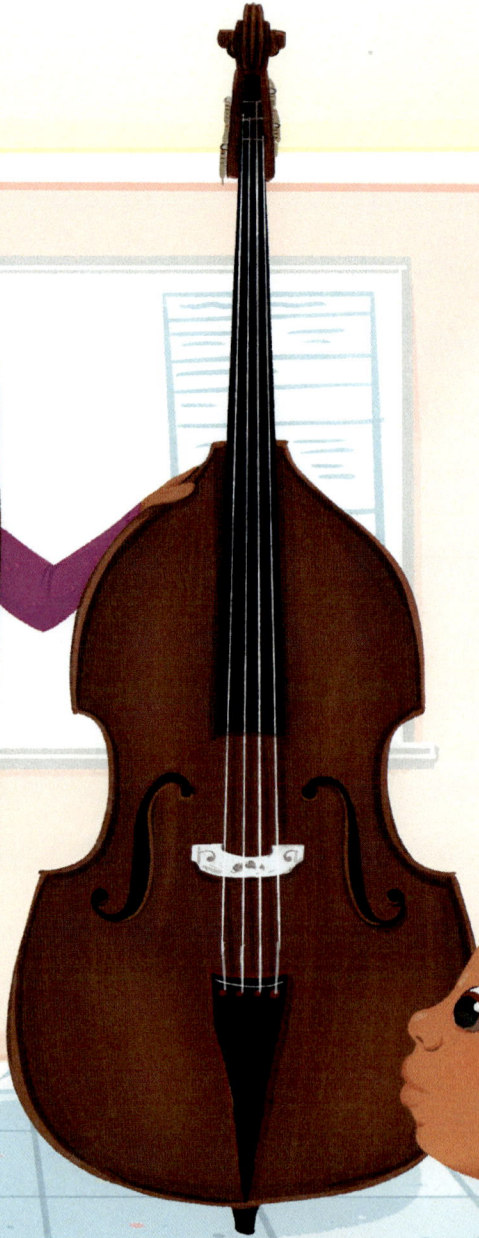

Standing in front of the class, Catalina takes a deep breath, turns around and positions herself next to the bass. All the students' eyes are wide with surprise at the size of the instrument.

"What is that thing?" she hears a couple of students whispering to each other.

She glances towards her teacher.

"Go ahead Catalina," says Ms. Narvaez with an encouraging nod.

Catalina clears her throat. "Good afternoon, everyone. Today I will be talking about my favorite instrument, the double bass," she begins, her voice shaking slightly.

"A what?" say some of the children in the classroom. Catalina pauses for a moment. She had worried that her classmates might not appreciate how incredible this instrument is, but she was determined to show them.

"A double bass," she repeats a little louder as she looks around the room and sees that everyone is looking at the bass with curiosity.

"People who play the double bass are called bassists," she manages to say after taking a big gulp.

She hears some of her classmates mumbling the unfamiliar words.

Catalina wonders if most of them have ever heard of or even seen her favorite instrument in the world. That is certainly going to change after today! She knows so much about the double bass and is eager to share her knowledge with her classmates.

Catalina raises her voice a little so that her classmates can refocus on her and says, "It is interesting that not all bassists call this instrument a double bass. Some call it an upright bass or a bass violin. It actually has several names," she says, biting her lip and looking over to her grandpa for help.

"It sure does have a lot of names," says her grandpa, raising his eyebrows while nodding. "The name it's called depends on the music being played with it," he adds as he looks over at Catalina sending her another encouraging wink so that she can continue.

"For example," Catalina begins again, "in classical music, many bassists call this a contrabass or string bass. In jazz or blues music, the musicians sometimes call it an upright bass. In bluegrass music, some musicians call it a bass fiddle."

A boy in the front, Jonathan, raises his hand and asks, "Why does it have so many names?"

"Well, that happened because this instrument has been played in many different types of music all over the world, and people just ended up giving it different names. But the most common name people use is simply the *Bass*," explains Catalina.

VIOLIN

VIOLA

CELLO

DOUBLE BASS

BOW

"It looks like a giant violin," blurts out Ingrid from the back of the room.

"That's because the violin and the double bass are both string instruments in the violin family. There is also a cello and a viola," Catalina explains as her grandpa opens up a poster to show the students. "As you can see, they are all similar, but the double bass is the biggest of them all," adds Catalina more confidently. "The violin can be held under the chin easily, but for the double bass, it requires strength to carry it around," she says, grunting jokingly, as she uses both her arms to easily lift the bass off the floor.

The kids in the class laugh. Catalina smiles, seeing that her classmates are enjoying her presentation.

She continues, "The main difference between these instruments is that they all have very different ranges in the sounds that they make. The double bass makes the lowest sound, while the violin makes the highest sound."

Her grandpa starts speaking in a low, deep voice saying, "You could say the double bass is like the low roar of a lion." Then he switches to a high-pitched voice, saying, "While a violin is like a little bird chirping in the morning." He flaps his hands in the air quickly and chirps!

All the students giggle at his imitation of a little bird.

"**N**ow, listen to the low sounds of these four strings," says Catalina as all the students lean forward, eager to hear. "This thick string is called the **E** string." She plucks the thickest string and a super low rumble fills the room. "This is what the second string sounds like. It's called the **A** string," she says as she plucks it and the class hears a rumble a little less deep.

"I can hear the difference!" some students say excitedly.

"And this is the **D** string," she says as she plucks the third string on the double bass. "And last but not least, is the thinnest string on the double bass. It's called the **G** string. This is what it sounds like," she says as she gives it a graceful pluck.

Another classmate, Cristian, raises his hand to ask a question. Catalina points to him.

"Catalina, when did you start playing the double bass?" he asks.

"Well, my mom and grandpa say I have been playing since I was in my mom's belly," she tells him as she giggles looking at her grandpa.

"It's true," he says. "Catalina would start moving around in her mom's belly every time I started to play my double bass! I know she was in there jamming away with me each time," he declares as he waves his finger at her.

Catalina's friend Alexander then asks, "How about after you were born? When did you start learning how to play the bass then?"

"Well, my grandpa has taught me since I was a little girl. I would help him pluck the strings at the bottom of the bass and he would move his hands up and down on the neck," she says as she points to the long upper portion of the bass. "But as I got older, I've been practicing more on my own because now I can reach up and down the neck all by myself," Catalina announces proudly. "I usually play pizzicato. That means to play with your fingers. But sometimes I play arco. That means to play with a bow," she says while pointing to what a bow looks like on the poster since, in her excitement, she left her bow this morning on her kitchen counter.

Next, April raises her hand and asks, "What kind of music can you play with a double bass?"

"All kinds of music! Jazz, classical, bluegrass, salsa, rock-n-roll and more," Catalina says with excitement. "In order to create music, you need different sounds and frequencies, and the deep sound of the bass is the foundation of it all. It's where it starts," Catalina explains matter-of-factly, feeling more confident in her presentation.

"So, is that your double bass?" asks Reid while shaking his hand in the air.

"This one is my grandpa's," says Catalina. "He's had it for over twenty-five years. It was originally made in Chicago in 1932!"

"**W**hoa!" say the students in shock. Catalina hears them whispering about how long ago that was.

"Yeah, it's ancient, almost a hundred years," she says, nodding in agreement with her classmates. "But last week I got to go to an awesome bass shop in Connecticut," she says with a huge grin on her face. "It's full of double basses and it's where my grandpa bought his bass too. The people who work there making the double basses are called Luthiers, and they are building a bass just for me."

"That's so cool!" she hears some classmates say.

"I can't wait until it's finished," she adds, smiling.

"Now, I will go over some parts of a double bass."

"First, this is the scroll," she says, rubbing her hand on the highest part of the bass for her classmates to see. "It is the usual decoration of the instrument and is like the signature of the luthier who made the bass."

Catalina moves her hand over to the side of the scroll and then continues, "These little metal knobs are called the tuners. You turn them back and forth to tune the strings." She twists the knobs to demonstrate.

"Tuning means to adjust the pitch, or how high or low the string sounds," she adds when she sees that some students look confused.

"Next, we have this long part here known as the neck." She runs her hand up and down the wooden stick underneath the scroll for her classmates to see. "You rest your thumb on the back of it while you press the strings down with your fingers on the front," she says as she demonstrates with her hand.

"This brings us to the next part," she says, raising her eyebrows, "the fingerboard. It is this long, dark piece attached to the neck, and this is where the strings are pushed down to change the pitch of the strings." Catalina demonstrates how they are pressed down onto the fingerboard.

"Hey, that's what I do on the guitar I play!" exclaims Nancy.

"Yeah it's similar to that," agrees Catalina.

She then puts one hand on the left side of the bass and the other on the right side of the bass. "These are known as the ribs or the sides of the bass. Some are more rounded like this one and others can be more pointed," she explains.

"Then we have this big area in the front of the bass that is called the top or table, and the back of a double bass is called, wait for it, the back," she says, smiling as she shrugs her shoulders. All the kids giggle.

"And, of course, these are the four strings I showed earlier. E, A, D, and G," she says, quickly pointing to each of them from thickest to thinnest.

"Can anyone guess what these holes on the top of the bass are called?" asks Catalina, pointing to the holes with each hand. She gives them a moment and hears the students whisper guesses, but no one dares to guess out loud. "They are called sound holes, but they are also known as F holes. Their job is to allow the sound to come out of the instrument."

"Ooohhh," she hears some of her classmates say at the same time.

"And last but not least, this is known as the bridge," she announces, pointing to the wooden arch between the sound holes. "Its job is to hold the strings in place."

Catalina looks at her grandpa, who says, "And now, it's time for some music."

"Yes, to end my presentation, I will play a piece I have practiced for a long time now," she says as she positions her body to the left of the bass, with one hand on the neck and the other where the fingerboard ends.

Catalina begins playing the double bass and the room immediately vibrates with mesmerizing sounds. Everyone is instantly captivated, smiling and looking at each other in awe. When she finishes, her classmates clap and cheer loudly.

Catalina takes a bow.

"Well done Catalina. Thank you for such a beautiful and informative presentation," says Ms. Narvaez, smiling.

Catalina's face beams with happiness and her heart now pounds with pride. All of her hard work with her grandpa has paid off. She really hopes she has sparked a love for playing music in her classmates, especially playing it with the best instrument in the whole wide world- the double bass!

How about you?
Would you like to play the double bass?

Meet The Author

Antonia Aviles grew up in the small town of South Fallsburg, NY, before moving to Kissimmee, FL, where she earned her Bachelor's Degree in Early Education and spent several years teaching elementary school.

Now living in Mystic, CT, she balances her love of writing with a passion for making homemade creations, gardening, and outdoor adventures. When she's not writing, you'll likely find her exploring nature, learning new languages, or traveling to new places.

Her debut children's books, **Jayla Spreads Loving Kindness** and **You Are Loved,** received awards from **Story Monsters Ink.** Antonia continues captivating young readers with her upcoming title, **Thea and Her Purple Dragon.**

Follow her literary journey on Instagram
@author_antonia_aviles

Made in the USA
Monee, IL
24 May 2025